Contents

Introduction

At the height of its power, the Roman Empire stretched from Britain in the west to Mesopotamia (modern Iraq) in the east. Rome itself was a wealthy city of a million people. A massive programme of building work had swept away the cramped, ugly tenement blocks and narrow, winding streets of the old city. Bridges had been built over the River Tiber. A system of aqueducts supplied water for fountains, homes and bath-houses. The imperial architects had created enormous buildings. The visitor could see such wonders as the great public baths, the awe-inspiring Forum built by the Emperor Trajan, the Colosseum, the Circus Maximus – which could seat 250,000 people – and the Pantheon with its magnificent dome.

The remains of the Colosseum in Rome.

Technology in the Time of
Ancient Rome

Robert Snedden

WAYLAND

Titles in the series

Ancient Egypt   **The Aztecs**

Ancient Greece   **The Maya**

Ancient Rome   **The Vikings**

Cover picture: A Roman surveyor using a *groma*.
Title page: A mosaic showing slaves pressing olives.
Contents page: A *ballista*, a Roman siege machine used for firing arrows.

Book editor: Alison Cooper
Series editor: Alex Woolf
Designers: Sterling Associates
Illustrator: Vana Haggerty
Cover illustrator: Adam Hook
Consultant: Jenny Hall, Museum of London
Production controller: Carol Stevens

First published in 1997 by
Wayland Publishers Ltd
61 Western Road, Hove
East Sussex, BN3 1JD

© Copyright 1997 Wayland Publishers Ltd

Find Wayland on the internet at http://www.wayland.co.uk

British Library Cataloguing in Publication Data
Snedden, Robert
Technology in the Time of Ancient Rome
1. Technology–Rome–Juvenile literature
I. Title II. Ancient Rome
609.3 '7

ISBN 0 7502 2064 3

Typeset by Sterling Associates
Printed and bound by G. Canale & C.S.p.A., Turin

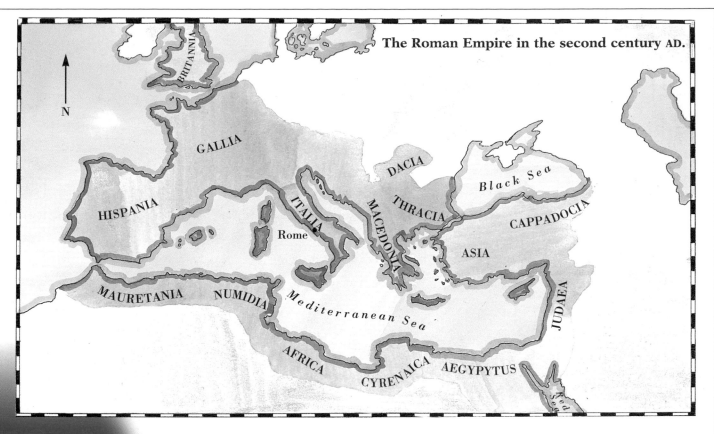

The Roman Empire in the second century AD.

Very few important inventions came from Rome. Much of the technology the Romans used had been invented by other civilizations, or in other parts of the Empire: the technique of glass-blowing was developed in Syria, for example. There seemed little point in inventing labour-saving devices when there was a ready supply of slaves to do the hard work. Yet although the Romans were not great inventors, they were excellent engineers. Many of their buildings, roads and bridges have long outlasted them, and survive to impress us today.

Working the land

The tools and techniques used in agriculture did not develop much during the Roman period. Farmers had no real need of labour-saving equipment because so many slaves were available to do the work cheaply. The tools these hard-pressed workers used were simple. They sowed seed by hand from baskets carried around their necks, and used a reaping hook or sickle for harvesting crops. Reaping was very hard work, although balancing the weight of the blade with the weight of the handle did make the sickle easier to use. In Roman times, the improved version of this tool became widespread.

The plough

The light plough, which was little more than a heavy pole drawn by a pair of oxen, had been in use for over 3,000 years before the Roman period. It was perfectly suited for use in the dry climates and light, crumbly soils of the Middle East and the Mediterranean area. In southern Italy, the Romans used a version of the light plough that was strengthened by adding an iron share to the cutting tip. Sometimes, they mounted the plough on wheels, to make it easier for the person guiding the oxen to manoeuvre it.

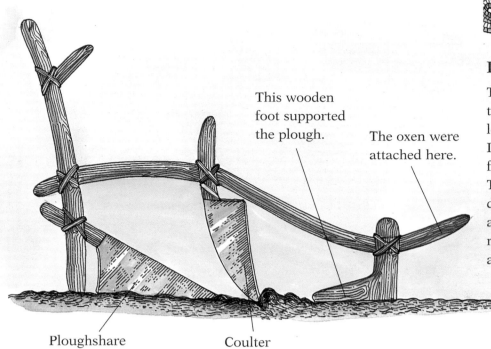

This wooden foot supported the plough.

The oxen were attached here.

Ploughshare

Coulter

Improving the plough

The light plough was of little use on the wet, sticky, clay soils of the lowland plains of northern Europe. It might have been the Romans who first improved it by adding a coulter. This was a heavy blade that hung down in front of the ploughshare and broke up the surface of the soil, making it easier to plough. Different attachments could be added to the basic plough, such as the *irpex*, a set of iron hooks that was used for tearing out roots and weeds.

Two tools in one

Another Roman innovation was to combine two tools in one. For example, a two-headed pick and spade could be used first to break up the soil and then to dig it. The hoe, which was used to keep down weeds, was combined with a mattock, used for loosening soil and roots. This mosaic shows a worker in a vineyard. Small pruning saws and a tool that was a combination of a knife blade and a spike were used for tending the vines. The Romans probably got the idea for this combined tool from the Greeks.

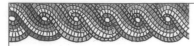

Bringing in the harvest

The harvest was of vital importance. Huge quantities of grain were needed to feed the population, and a great deal was imported to Rome from other parts of the Empire, particularly North Africa. At harvest time, landowners would hire extra workers to help their slaves to bring in the crop and store the grain. A reaping machine, called a *vallus*, was invented in the Roman province of Gaul (now France), probably in the first century AD. It meant that fewer workers were needed to bring in the harvest, but the vallus was never widely used. Landowners who had plenty of slaves were probably content to go on using them instead.

The *vallus*

The *vallus* had a closely-spaced row of sharp prongs fitted to the front of a frame. As it was pushed along by a donkey, the prongs gripped the stalks. A hopper, rather like the grass-collecting box on a lawnmower, caught the heads of grain as they were thrown into the air.

Once they had harvested the crop, the workers had to separate the grain from the chaff, the unwanted parts of the plant. One way to do this was by using a *tribulum*, a heavy wooden sledge drawn by oxen. It was studded on the bottom with flints or nails that pressed the grain out from the chaff. The 'Punic cart', which originally came from North Africa, was an improvement. As it was dragged over the harvested crop by donkeys or asses, its toothed rollers revolved, pressing out the grain. The cart also had a seat for a driver, whose weight helped to press the rollers down on to the grain.

Winnowing

The farm workers removed the chaff from the threshed grain by winnowing. Often, they used a shallow winnowing basket like this one. As the worker shook the basket from side to side, the lighter chaff blew away and the heavier grain settled in the bottom.

Storing the grain

The Romans had to protect their grain from damp, which made it rot, and from vermin. In damper climates, they dried it before it was stored. This was done by spreading it out on a drying floor, heated by a *hypocaust*, a type of underfloor heating that we will look at on page 18. The granaries in which the grain was stored were long narrow buildings with floors raised on wooden or stone supports. The supports can be seen in this picture of the remains of the granary at Corbridge, in Northumberland. The surface of the inner walls was sealed with *amurca*. This gave off a horrible smell, which might have deterred vermin. The grain itself was probably kept in bins, lined up on either side of a central passageway.

Milling

The Romans ground their grain into flour by crushing it between large stones. Families used millstones that they turned by hand to grind grain for their own use, but when flour was needed in larger quantities, animal or water power was used to turn the millstones. The flour that was produced was rather coarse, so it had to be sifted before it could be used for baking. The sifters were made of fine horsehair or linen. They trapped any partially-ground grains and let the flour fall through into the large jars in which it was stored.

The donkey mill

In a donkey mill, a donkey was attached to a millstone by a beam. As the donkey walked round and round, it turned the millstone.

The hollow outer millstone was turned by the donkey.

Grain was fed into the mill.

Inner millstone

The grain was crushed as it fell between the millstones.

The flour collected at the bottom.

The water wheel

The invention of the water wheel by the famous architect and engineer Vitruvius, in the first century BC, is one of the few examples of the Romans harnessing natural energy other than muscle power. The wheels were mainly used to turn millstones, and the largest Roman water-mill was built at Barbégal, in France, in about AD 300. The engineers directed water from an aqueduct down two streams that each fell through eight levels. On each level there was a water wheel turning a millstone, making sixteen mills in all. This massive mill complex could grind enough grain in a single day to feed over 12,000 people.

A series of gears connected the wheel to a millstone, turning the vertical spinning motion of the wheel into horizontal spin.

Water was collected in a millpond and directed to hit the top of the wheel.

The undershot wheel

A wheel was placed in the middle of a stream or river. The force of the water rushing past it spun the wheel.

The paddles carried the water down the wheel.

The overshot wheel

The undershot wheel did not work when the water level in the river was too high or too low. The overshot wheel provided a solution to this problem, although it was more difficult to build. It produced energy up to eight times more efficiently.

Making a Roman recipe

The last stage in producing food is, of course, to bake something with the flour. This is a Roman recipe for a sweet cheesecake that you might like to try.

Heat the oven to 220°C/425°F/Gas Mark 7. Sift 120 g of plain flour into a bowl. Beat 225 g of ricotta cheese until it is soft and then stir it into the flour. Add a beaten egg and stir the mixture until a soft dough has formed. Divide the dough into four and shape each piece into a bun. Place each bun on a greased baking tray with a fresh bay leaf under each one. Bake the cakes in the oven for 35–40 minutes until they are golden brown. Warm 120 g of clear honey and place the warm cakes in it so that they soak it up. Leave the cakes for about 30 minutes before serving them.

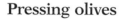

Oil and wine

Apart from grain, the two crops of greatest importance to the Romans were olives, which were used to make oil, and grapes, for making wine. A rubbish dump discovered near Rome gives some idea of the scale of olive-oil production: it contained about 40 million pots that had been used for carrying oil. Slaves picked the olives by hand, or brought them down from the trees by hitting the branches gently. At the oil factory, they were lightly pressed, so that as many stones as possible could be removed. This was important, because they gave the oil a bitter taste. Special olive mills, designed to avoid crushing any stones that were left, were used to crush the flesh. The oil was then squeezed out of the pulped flesh in a press.

The Romans learned from the Greeks how to grow vines and make wine. They spread wine-growing throughout their Empire, finding different varieties of grape to suit the different climates and conditions in far-flung provinces. They even managed to grow a variety that would thrive in the cool British climate.

Pressing olives

The Romans used several different types of press. The simple lever press was brought down on the olives with considerable force by pulling on a rope wound around a cylinder, as shown in this mosaic. The oil that was pressed out ran through channels in the stone floor to be collected in tanks.

Making wine

Ripe grapes were taken to large vats for crushing. Sometimes, the Romans did this very simply by treading the grapes and using large rods to help crush them. Another option was to use a screw press, like the one below.

A screw press

The screw was turned to bring the board down on to the grapes and press them.

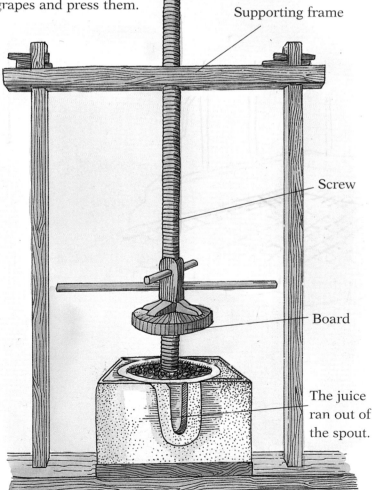

Supporting frame

Screw

Board

The juice ran out of the spout.

Transporting the wine

After the grapes had been pressed, the juice was strained from them and collected in large pottery jars, where it was left for ninety days to ferment. It was then sold, and sometimes transported in large quantities over long distances. In Italy, it was usually carried in an ox skin, mounted on the frame of a wagon. Sometimes, it was measured into amphorae, like the ones shown here. These large pottery jars could be sealed and stacked together safely for transport by road or sea, and might hold as much as a thousand litres of wine.

Clothing

Sheep's wool was the main fibre used for making textiles in western Europe, and many of the clothes worn by the Romans were made of wool. The Romans also grew flax, from which they made linen. Sometimes, they produced very fine linen with threads of gold woven into it.

They made leather clothes from the skins of animals, such as cattle, goats and deer. The skins of sheep were also used, although this was less common. Before the skins could be worn, they had to be treated to make them supple and to prevent them from rotting. This process is called tanning. The Romans tanned the skins by soaking them in a solution of alum and salt, or by using natural chemicals that are found in bark, wood, leaves and fruits.

Shearing and spinning

The Romans used iron shears, like the ones shown here, to shear their sheep. They spun the wool with a hand spindle, which was spun like a top to draw the fibres into a tight yarn. It is actually possible to tell which part of the Empire a piece of cloth came from by looking at the way the thread turns. In the western provinces, it was the custom to spin the spindle clockwise, whereas in the east it was spun in the opposite direction.

The warp threads were wound around poles at each end. Loom weights kept the warp threads taut.

The weft thread was passed under and over the warp threads. It was then brought back again and the process was repeated until the cloth was complete.

Weaving and fulling

The spun thread was woven into cloth on an upright wooden loom. Before the cloth could be used, it had to be treated to remove dirt and natural oils from the wool. The workers who did this were called fullers. They soaked the cloth in cold water, to which fuller's earth, a very absorbent clay-like substance, had been added. Sometimes, they soaked the cloth in urine instead. The fullers would also beat the cloth, to improve its texture and bulk. Then it would be washed, bleached or dyed and pressed, ready for making up into clothes.

Making a toga

The toga was the garment worn by Roman citizens. It was made from a single semi-circular piece of wool or linen. Try making your own toga from an old sheet (make sure it is old before cutting it up!). You might need someone to help you put it on.

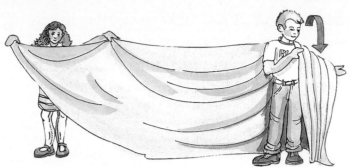

1 Tie a belt around your waist and then drape one end of the toga over your left shoulder so that it touches the floor.

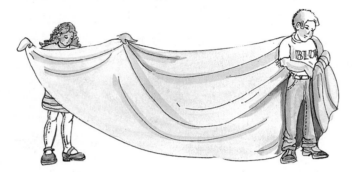

2 Tuck some of the material into your belt at your left hip.

3 Take hold of the back of the toga and make several pleats in it as you fold it in towards you.

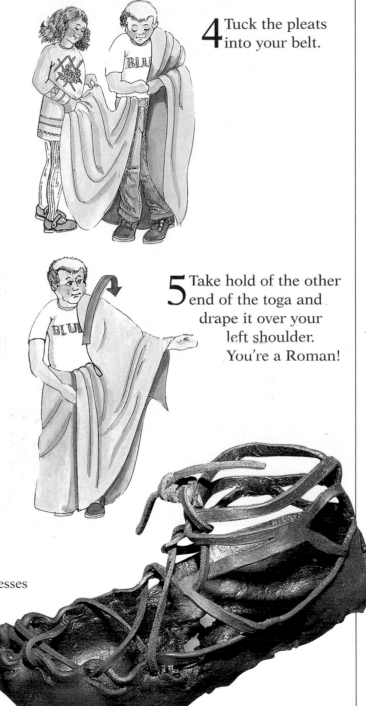

4 Tuck the pleats into your belt.

5 Take hold of the other end of the toga and drape it over your left shoulder. You're a Roman!

Leather

The Romans used leather made from cattle skins for harnesses and footwear. Footwear ranged from the nail-studded shoes and sandals worn by soldiers, to very delicate slippers, often dyed in different colours. Leather made from goat skins was used to make clothing, tents and bags.

Building to last

The most popular building material available to the early Romans was mud brick, strengthened by timber. Later, they used a soft volcanic rock called tufa, and later still, the stronger travertine stone was used. To begin with, large rectangular blocks of stone were held together by mortar. As the quality of the mortar improved, smaller, more irregularly-shaped stones were used.

In central Italy in the second century BC, the Romans developed a new approach to building. They discovered how to make an unusually strong cement, using a volcanic dust called *pozzolana*, mixed with lime. Using this cement to make concrete produced a hard and adaptable building material, which the Romans soon began to use in preference to traditional materials. At first, they combined the concrete with rubble to form the insides of walls, but gradually they began to use it on its own, as they realized that it was cheaper and much stronger than stone. After the great fire that devastated Rome in AD 64, the city was largely rebuilt in concrete faced with brick.

Carpentry

Many of the tools used by Roman carpenters, such as the chisels shown here, were similar to those used today. Several improvements to the design of saws were introduced by the Romans. They made a saw that could be pushed and pulled. They also invented the frame saw, in which the blade was fixed to wooden uprights joined by a crossbar. A variety of frame saws were produced, including large saws that were operated by two people.

Building a concrete wall

Builders made a wall in stages, setting up a new level of scaffolding when the wall became too high for them to work on. They often laid a layer of large bricks through the wall when they had finished each stage, to prevent the concrete from sinking down the wall cavity too much. Outside Italy, the concrete was often of poor quality and it was necessary to add layers of bricks for added strength.

Wooden frames were inserted to hold in the concrete below ground level. (These were removed once the concrete had set.)

A stiff concrete mixture was shovelled into the cavity.

Bricks or stones were built up on each side to form a cavity.

The wall was supported by wooden scaffolding until the concrete had hardened.

Freedom to build

The great value of concrete was that it could be poured into and over timber frameworks, making difficult constructions, such as vaults, much easier to build. More and more daring and complex buildings went up in Rome in the first and second centuries AD, as concrete vaults and domes were made in baths, palaces, temples and other public buildings. The concrete walls were usually faced with baked bricks, smooth, irregularly-shaped stones, or square stones set on edge to form a network pattern. These are the ruins of the Basilica Nova in Rome, which has three vaults rising to a height of almost 35 m.

The comforts of home

In Rome, most people lived in tenement blocks. Many of these were badly constructed and, often, they burned down or collapsed. Disease spread easily in the overcrowded living conditions. Outside Rome, especially in the northern parts of the Empire, poorer people lived in timber-framed houses. These had walls made of mud brick, or of wattle and daub.

By contrast, the town house of a well-off Roman citizen could be lavish. Grand dining halls and sitting rooms surrounded a central garden. Ornate furniture, fine mosaics and sculptures filled the house. Some houses even had glass in the windows. The Romans were probably the first to use glass for this purpose, especially in the north. However, it was a luxury that few people could afford.

Central heating

The Romans used *hypocausts*, the earliest known form of central heating, to heat large houses and the public baths. *Hypocausts* provided effective underfloor heating, but only the most important rooms would be heated in this way. Other rooms might be kept warm by burning charcoal in braziers.

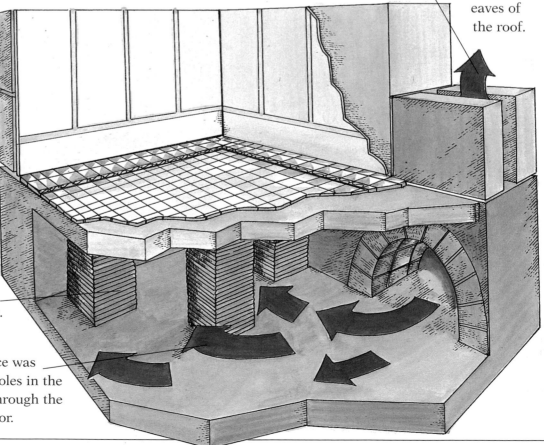

Flues in the walls allowed warm air to circulate and then to escape under the eaves of the roof.

The floor of the room was supported on stacks of clay tiles.

Hot air from a furnace was fed through arched holes in the wall and circulated through the space beneath the floor.

Under lock and key

The Romans were just as keen to protect their homes and possessions as we are. They produced the first rotary locks, similar to the locks we use today, in which the key is turned in the lock. The locks were made of iron and the keys of bronze. The Romans also invented padlocks. The bolt of the padlock was tipped with springs that opened out inside the case when the bolt was pushed in. A key had to be inserted in the bottom of the case to squeeze the springs together, allowing the bolt to be pulled back out again.

Mosaics

The floors and walls of Roman buildings were often decorated with mosaics. These patterns or pictures were made from small cubes of stone, tile, glass and pottery called *tesserae*. The person making the mosaic would spread fine mortar over a section of the wall or floor – a thicker layer was used on the floor, to create a waterproof barrier. Before the mortar dried, guidelines were drawn on to it, and the *tesserae* were pressed in to form part of the picture. When the mosaic was complete, it was smoothed and polished. Often, sections of mosaic were made up in a workshop and carried to the building in trays to be fixed into place.

Making a mosaic

You might like to try making your own version of a Roman mosaic. You can use small squares of coloured card instead of stones and mortar. You also need some paste or glue, and a large piece of card on which to stick the mosaic pieces. Plan your design before you start, so that you know where to stick things down. The more detailed you want your mosaic to be, the smaller the pieces you will have to use. Perhaps you could try to do a mosaic of something in this book, such as the Pont du Gard on page 27.

Public buildings

Roman engineers were extraordinarily skilful, and they mastered the difficult technique of constructing stone arches. Buildings that are constructed using arches put much less strain on stone and make it a far more efficient building material. The Romans used arches in the building of their bridges and aqueducts, so this technique was vital to the development of the road network and the water system. They adapted the same building principle to enable them to construct vaults and domes.

This arch once formed part of the Roman bath-house in the city of Dougga in Tunisia.

Building an arch

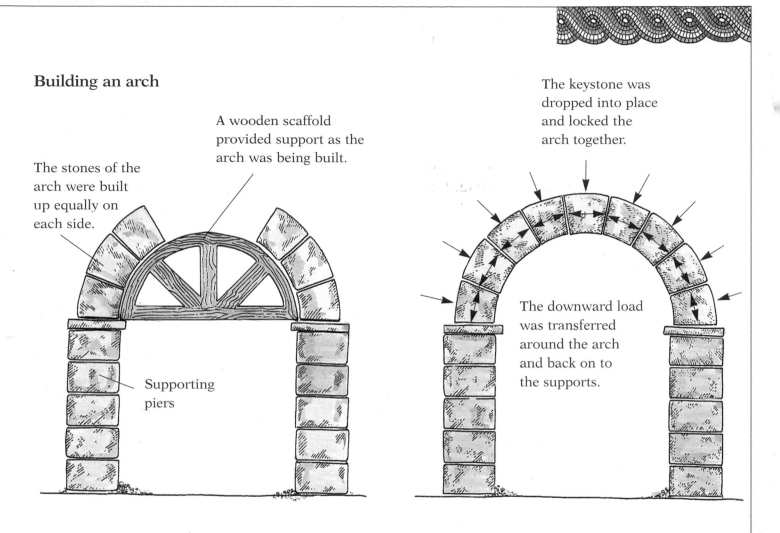

The stones of the arch were built up equally on each side.

A wooden scaffold provided support as the arch was being built.

Supporting piers

The keystone was dropped into place and locked the arch together.

The downward load was transferred around the arch and back on to the supports.

The Pantheon

The Pantheon, the shrine of all the gods, in Rome is the largest and best-preserved example of a solid concrete dome from the ancient world. The building that survives today dates from the time of the Emperor Hadrian and was built between AD 118 and AD 125. The foundations are over 7 m thick. The lower walls were made of concrete mixed with travertine, a tough stone that was quarried near Rome.

The dome itself was built of layer upon layer of concrete. The concrete was mixed with lightweight rocks – tufa and pumice – to make it as light as possible, but it still weighed more than 5,000 tonnes. Brick arches were used to support the weight of the concrete while it was setting. The inside of the dome is 42 m high, equal to its inner diameter. Until the twentieth century, this was the largest dome ever constructed.

Roads and bridges

The Romans were great road builders – by early in the fourth century AD, their engineers had constructed a network of 85,000 km of roads. This network, spreading out like a web from Rome, was vital to the survival of the Empire. Along these roads, messengers travelled swiftly, covering at least 80 km a day. More importantly, troops could reach trouble spots quickly to stamp out revolts.

The first major road was built to link Rome with the town of Capua, to the south, and it was begun in 312 BC. It became known as the Appian Way, one of the Empire's greatest roads, and it eventually ran from Rome to the port of Brindisi in south-eastern Italy.

The exact method the Romans used to construct a road varied, according to the kind of ground the road was being laid on. Roads across marshy areas, for example, 'floated' on wooden rafts. Sand and stone were put down in layers to form the foundations, and paving stones were laid on top. Roads were built with a camber, to allow water to drain off the surface into ditches at each side.

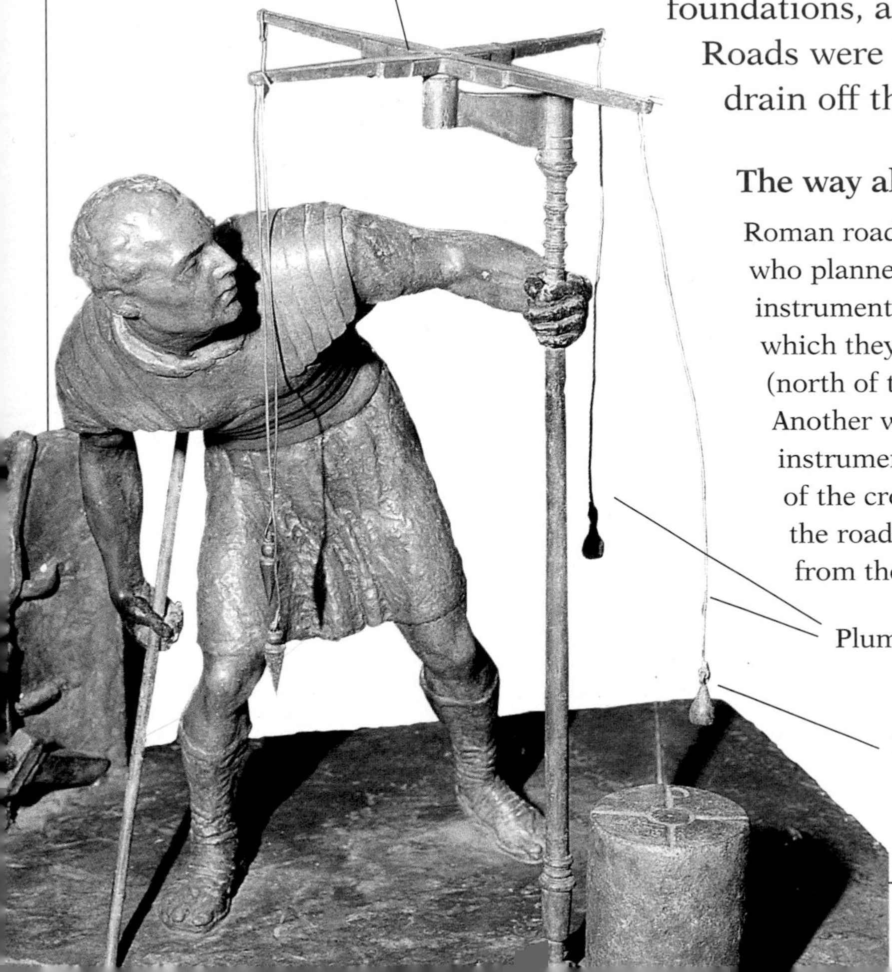

Crosspieces

Plumb lines

Lead weights

The way ahead

Roman roads are famous for being straight. The surveyors who planned the course of the roads had several instruments to help them. One was a portable sundial, which they could use to plot the direction of the road (north of the Equator, the sun is due south at midday). Another was the *groma*, shown here. They used this instrument to check right angles. By looking along one of the crosspieces, they could also check that the line of the road was straight. The word 'plumb line' comes from the Roman word for lead, *plumbum*, which was used for the weights on the *groma*.

Making a *groma*

To make your own *groma*, you will need two pieces of wood to use as crosspieces, a set square, a hammer and nails, four equal lengths of thread or string, four small screw hooks and four weights. Lots of things will work well as weights: try using keys, bulldog clips or metal nuts. They need to be things that you can tie on easily. You also need a pole that is about the same height as you – you could try using a broom handle.

1 Nail the two crosspieces together at right angles to each other (use your set square to check the angles). Screw a hook to each end.

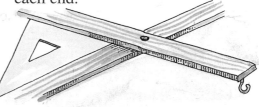

2 Tie a weight to each hook using thread or string. Make sure the weights can dangle freely and that the strings are all the same length.

3 Push the pole into the ground and fix the *groma* to the top of it. When the weights are all hanging level with each other, the *groma* is level. Try using it to check a straight line.

Sights

Gears

The *dioptra*

Roman surveyors probably also used the *dioptra*. This was invented in the first century AD by the great engineer Hero of Alexandria, who was known as the 'Machine Man'. The surveyor would use the sophisticated gear system to turn the sights on the circular metal plate, to align them with a sighting rod held some distance away. Using this tool, he could work out heights and angles. It was the forerunner of the modern theodolite.

Bridges and viaducts

The Romans had the engineering expertise, wealth and labour force required to build the finest bridges in the ancient world. Bridges were a vital part of their road network. They built smaller bridges of wood, and none of these have survived, but some of their larger ones still stand, nearly 2,000 years after they were built.

It was the Romans' skill in the technique of building arches that made such magnificent feats of engineering possible. Because the arches of a bridge were built one at a time, the piers had to be wide enough to take the weight of an arch at one side without being pushed over. Once the bridge was completed, the weight was distributed more evenly.

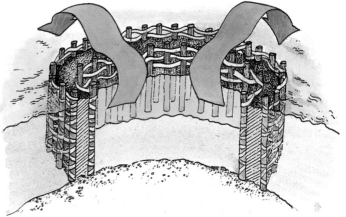

Coffer dams

Some of the Roman bridges that survive today have piers built on solid rock foundations. The Romans also devised timber coffer dams that allowed them to construct piers in midstream. The *pozzolana* concrete was ideal for bridges, because it was waterproof. The Romans used it to construct bridge foundations below the water level.

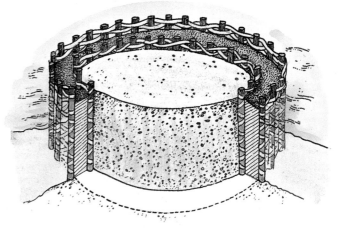

1 Two concentric rings of wooden piles were driven into the riverbed around the site of the pier. The piles were laced with wickerwork and the gap between the piles was filled with clay.

2 The water inside the rings was drained, by pumping or bailing it out.

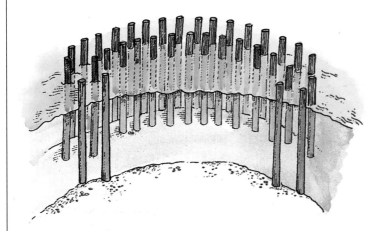

3 Then the exposed riverbed was dug out, and the pier was built on the dry surface.

The Ponte Sant' Angelo across the River Tiber in Rome was built on coffer-dam foundations over 1,800 years ago.

The crane

Roman engineers used cranes powered by animals or slaves to lift the heavy blocks needed to build bridges. They also used cranes in harbours for loading and unloading ships. A simple crane consisted of a pulley at the top of a pole, which was anchored by guy ropes. A larger crane would consist of a system of pulleys and winches.

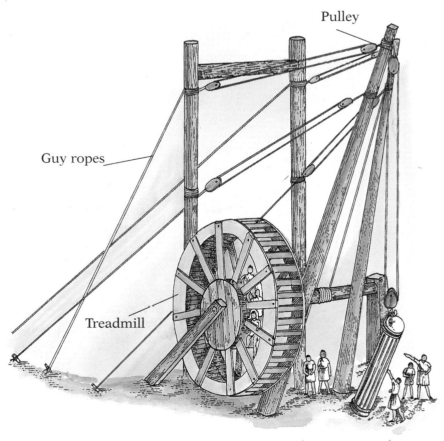

Pulley

Guy ropes

Treadmill

Making a pulley

Cranes can lift heavy loads because they use pulleys. Running a rope or cable around a pulley allows you to pull an object up while you pull down. Pulleys can also be used to increase the force produced by your effort. Try making your own pulley to lift a load.

1 Attach a cotton reel to a load. This is the lower pulley.

2 Attach a second cotton reel to a support. This is the upper pulley.

3 Tape a long piece of string to the upper pulley. Run the string round the lower pulley and back over the upper pulley.

4 Pull on the end of the string to raise the load.

Supplying water

Aqueducts

A supply of fresh water is essential for the health of any community. In a small town, people could usually get all the water they needed from streams or wells. But as Roman cities grew in both size and complexity, it became necessary to set up a more sophisticated way of supplying water.

As early as 312 BC, the Romans began to construct aqueducts to supply water to Rome. These systems of channels and bridges were not a Roman invention. An aqueduct 50 km long had been built around 400 years earlier, to carry water to the city of Nineveh in ancient Assyria, and there were other examples. However, the engineers of Rome skilfully combined reservoir construction, bridge-building, road-making, tunnelling and piping to make the finest water system of the ancient world.

The Aqua Claudia

Aqueducts used gravity to move water from a distant source to wherever it was needed: as in a natural stream or river, the water had to flow downhill to keep moving. The Aqua Claudia, built in AD 47, supplied Rome from a source 70 km away. The source was just 250 m higher than Rome itself. This meant that the aqueduct had to drop no more than 1 m in height for every 280 m of its length. Otherwise, the water would have stopped flowing as it levelled out. Most of the Aqua Claudia ran underground. This was partly to protect the water from being contaminated, either accidentally or deliberately.

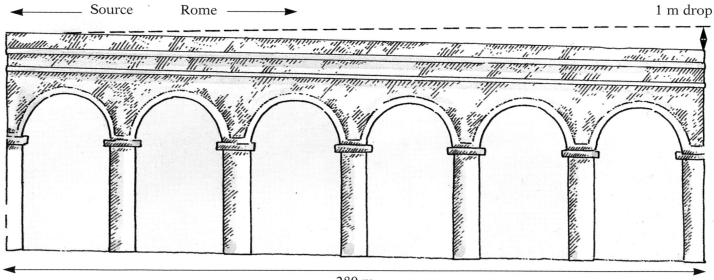

The Pont du Gard

The Pont du Gard in France, which still stands today, is a superb example of the skill and ingenuity of the Roman engineers. It was completed in AD 14 after 35 years of work. The blocks from which it is built fit together so tightly that no cement or mortar is needed to hold them in place. Some of the largest blocks weigh 6 tonnes or more, but the Romans had no powerful motorized winches to haul them into position. Instead, they used cranes powered by slaves on treadmills to do the work.

Making an aqueduct

You will need cardboard tubes such as those from the inside of kitchen rolls, some drinking straws, a yoghurt pot, sticky tape, scissors and some salt or sugar.

1 Tape the tubes together to make an 'aqueduct'.

2 Glue or tape the straws to make triangular supports for the aqueduct. Make sure each support is slightly smaller than the previous one, so that the aqueduct slopes.

3 Sprinkle the salt or sugar (the 'water') down the aqueduct. It should 'flow' along it. You may need to make the slope steeper or gentler to get a steady flow.

4 Direct the 'water' into a 'settling tank' made from a clean yoghurt pot. Try making holes in the pot and taping on smaller tubes made from straws to act as pipes. See if you can keep the 'water' flowing through the pipes.

Pipes, baths and drains

Once the water from the aqueduct reached the town, it poured into a settling tank. From there, large lead pipes carried it to different parts of the town. Smaller pipes made of lead, wood or terracotta fed water to the public fountains, the bath-houses and the homes of those rich enough to have water piped in directly.

The Romans were very keen on cleanliness, and scarcely a town in the Empire was without its baths. Several of the emperors, including Augustus, Nero, Caracalla and Diocletian, built great public baths in Rome itself. These were huge structures with towering concrete vaults, richly decorated with paintings, sculptures and mosaics. Most bath-houses followed the same general plan. The four main rooms were the undressing room, the cold room, the warm room and the hot room. As well as hot, tepid and cool baths, there were rooms where people could meet friends or take exercise.

Public toilets

More water per person flowed into ancient Rome than into present-day New York. Few houses were equipped with stopcocks, so the water ran continuously, as it did through the bath-houses and fountains. This meant that an efficient drainage system was essential. Excess water from the bath-houses was used to flush the public toilets, which had a row of seats over a channel of running water. It seems that the Romans did not mind someone else sitting next to them!

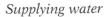

Sewers

Roman cities had elaborate underground sewage systems. The Cloaca Maxima in Rome was built in the third century BC to drain the Forum. It is still in use today, and this picture shows an outlet from the sewer into the River Tiber.

Hot baths

The water supply to the Roman bath-houses was sufficient for thousands of visitors each day. The rooms were heated by hot air, which was pumped under the floors and through the walls of the bathing areas, so that the baths could remain open even during the winter. These are the remains of the Roman baths at Bath in England. At the front of the picture, you can see the lead-lined channel that carried hot water to the bath.

Mining

The Romans used many different metals, including gold, silver, lead and iron. All of these had to be mined. Wherever possible, they dug out the metals from the surface, but often a rich vein of ore had to be followed underground.

Conditions for the miners were often appalling. This was a job that was usually done by slaves and criminals, for whom being sent to the mines was scarcely better than a death sentence. The tunnels in which they worked might be little more than a metre high. Oil lamps provided the light, but these used up oxygen and made breathing difficult. The miners split the rock by setting a fire and then dousing it with vinegar. The sudden change in temperature shattered the rock, but the smell added to the unpleasantness of the working conditions.

Going down a mine

Roman mines could be surprisingly extensive, with tunnels over 1,000 m long at a depth of 200 m or more beneath the surface. The miners were lowered down the deep shafts using a winch. Shallower shafts might have hand- and footholds cut into the walls so that the miners could climb down.

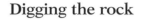

Digging the rock

The miners used stone and metal picks and shovels to dig the rock, and they carried the ore back to the surface in baskets made of copper or woven grass.

3 It was scooped up by the second wheel. The process continued until the water reached the surface.

Flooding

Flooding was a constant problem in the mines. The Romans tackled the problem by using water wheels. At the Río Tinto mine in Spain, they built eight pairs of wheels to lift the water over 30 m to the surface, where it was drained off. The wheels were turned by slaves walking them round like treadmills.

2 The water was emptied into a channel on the next level.

1 Water was scooped up in the bucket-shaped paddles and carried up the wheel.

Lowest level of mine

Metal-working

The Romans used a number of different methods for extracting pure metals from ores. The furnaces used to smelt iron ore burned charcoal, and foot bellows were used to make them as hot as possible. Although they reached temperatures of around 1,300 °C, they were still not hot enough to produce fully molten iron. A small ball of iron would form at the bottom of the furnace, and this was taken out and hammered into a bar of wrought iron.

To make iron stronger, the Romans reheated it between layers of charcoal. Charcoal contains carbon, and when this is combined with iron, it forms steel. Additional heating and hammering of the steel-coated iron produced high-quality blades. It is most likely that the secret of steel production came to the West from India, and when the Roman Empire came to an end, the secret was lost for almost a thousand years.

The blacksmith

Just about every town in the Empire must have had at least one blacksmith. With his hammer, anvil and pincers, the blacksmith made the pots and tools that local people required. He would heat ingots of iron until they were red-hot and then hammer them into the required shape on the anvil. He reheated the worked iron as often as necessary until the object was finished.

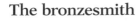

Casting in bronze

1 A model of the object was made in wax.

2 The model was coated in clay.

3 The clay was heated until the wax melted and ran out, leaving a mould.

4 Molten bronze was poured into the mould.

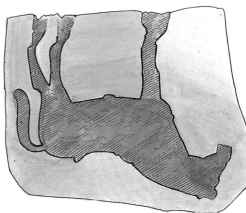

5 When the bronze had set solid, the cast was broken open to reveal the bronze object inside.

The bronzesmith

Bronze was used for a number of everyday objects, and there were almost as many bronzesmiths as blacksmiths. Many bronze objects were made by casting. Smaller items were made using the method described here, but it would have been too expensive to make larger items in solid bronze. Large items were usually hollow, or had a clay core.

These Roman bells are made of bronze.

Crafts

Skilled craftspeople would make and sell all kinds of goods from workshops that were part of their homes. They used bronze and other metals to make a wide range of small objects, such as simple household utensils. Wealthier customers could buy elegant vessels of gold and silver, often engraved with decorations. Terracotta – an unglazed, brownish-red type of pottery – was popular for lamps and other items. A thriving glassware industry developed in the later years of the Roman Empire.

Various metals were used for making jewellery. Iron was used to make rings, and mixing copper with zinc produced a gold-coloured metal that was used as a substitute for real gold. Goldsmiths were highly respected craftspeople. They made sheets of gold by hammering an ingot until it was very thin, and then made the gold sheets into brooches and pendants. Gold wire was formed by rolling a strip of the metal between plates made of stone or bronze. It was used to make rings, earrings and ornamental chains.

Decorating jewellery

Goldsmiths used delicate chisels to make decorations on the surface of the metal, or hammered it at the back to make a decoration that stood out at the front. Precious stones such as emeralds and sapphires, or coloured glass, could be set into grooves cut in the surface of the gold.

People had known how to make glass since the time of the ancient Middle Eastern civilizations, 2,500 years before the Roman Empire, but glass-making developed considerably in Roman times. Glass-blowing was invented in around 30 BC, possibly in Syria. Someone discovered that it was possible to shape molten glass by blowing air into it with a hollow metal tube, or blowpipe. The discovery spread rapidly throughout the Empire.

Making glass

Glass was made using a mixture of silica, soda and lime. The Romans heated the mixture in a furnace to drive off impurities, and then heated it again, in a clay crucible, to a temperature of 1,100–1,200 °C. This produced molten glass, which could then be shaped in a mould or by blowing it. Enormous numbers of glass vessels were produced for a variety of purposes, including containers for cosmetics, drinking vessels, jars and dishes. The Romans even recycled their glass, by melting it down again and producing new vessels.

Glass-blowing

1 The glass-maker blew down a hollow metal tube to produce a bubble of molten glass.

2 The glass bubble was rolled over another tube to shape the neck of the wine glass.

3 A second tube was inserted at the other end, and the first tube was twisted off.

4 While the glass was still soft, the base of the wine glass was shaped.

5 The top of the glass was hollowed out.

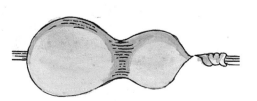

Medicine

Medical schools as we know them did not exist in the ancient world, although many doctors learned their skills as boy apprentices to other doctors. In the army, soldiers who became ill or were wounded in battle were cared for by the medics attached to their units.

Roman doctors tackled surprisingly delicate and dangerous operations, such as the removal of cataracts. Cataracts cause the lens of the eye to become clouded, and this can eventually make the sufferer blind. The Romans used fine needles set inside thin tubes to treat this condition. The tube would be inserted into the lens, and the doctor would use the needle to break up the cataract. Having done that, he would remove the needle and use the tube to suck out the pieces of cataract. A more common treatment was to use a plain needle to push the cataract to the bottom of the eye, out of the way.

As early as 300 BC, the Romans were making artificial legs to replace limbs lost in accidents or battle. Thin sheets of bronze were wrapped around a piece of wood shaped to resemble the leg, and a wooden foot was attached at the base.

A Roman surgeon

This relief is from the funeral monument of a surgeon. The symbol of a snake was often used to identify people whose work was connected with medicine; you can see one here, curling through the tree.

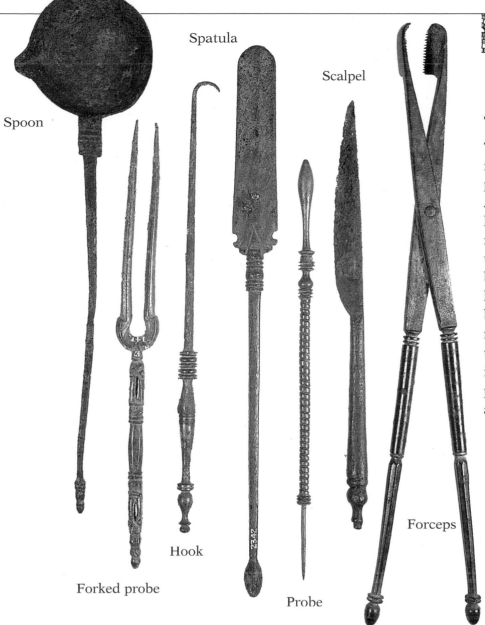

Spoon

Spatula

Scalpel

Forked probe

Hook

Probe

Forceps

Tools of the trade

The finest Roman medical instruments would not look out of place in a modern doctor's surgery. As well as the instruments shown here, a Roman doctor's equipment might also have included fine-toothed saws, for cutting through bone, and surgical scissors and knives. They were often made of bronze, as this was a practical and relatively cheap material from which to produce intricate surgical instruments. The best doctors preferred instruments made of a fine-quality steel from Austria.

A hole in the head

One of the most extraordinary items in the Roman medical kit was the drill used for trepanation. This procedure, apparently practised by many peoples since at least 6,000 BC, involves drilling holes in the skull. A bow was used to spin the drill, which pressed down into the patient's skull. The Romans seem to have believed that the treatment relieved pain in the head caused by wounds or disease.

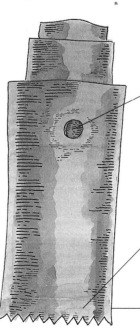

The bow string was threaded through the hole.

The drill was pressed into the patient's skull.

Transport

Travelling the roads

Travelling on land was made much easier by the network of roads for which the Romans are famous. Those who needed to travel quickly, such as couriers carrying messages across the Empire, would travel by horse. The Emperor Augustus set up a series of rest stations or inns every 10–20 km along the roads, where his couriers could be sure of finding fresh horses. This allowed them to cover up to 80 km a day. Roman riders used harnesses that were similar to those used today, but they did not have stirrups. Although the stirrup had been invented in India in the second century BC, it did not reach Europe for almost a thousand years.

Transporting goods

Pack animals, such as donkeys, were used to carry goods. Loads that were too heavy to be carried on donkey-back were transported on wagons, pulled by mules or oxen. The Romans also used a four-wheeled carriage, called a *raeda*, to transport heavy loads. It could carry goods weighing over 300 kg, and it was pulled by teams of eight or ten mules, harnessed two abreast.

Carrying passengers

The *raeda* could be used with horses, too, as a fast passenger vehicle, carrying a driver and passenger. The passenger version is shown in this picture. A two-wheeled *cisium* was also used for fast journeys. It was a light carriage for one or two passengers that was pulled by mules or ponies.

The litter

Well-to-do people might travel in a litter. This was a chair suspended from two horizontal poles and carried by men or animals. The litter was probably introduced into Europe from Asia and was used by the ancient Assyrians, Babylonians and Greeks, as well as the Romans. Litters, carried by two or four men, horses or mules, were usually designed to transport only one person at a time. It was probably the most comfortable way to get around – for the person in the chair.

Travelling by sea

It was cheaper, and often more convenient, to move large cargoes by sea rather than overland, and most of Rome's trade was carried out by way of the sea. As with so much else, slave labour was used for the time-consuming and expensive work of building ships. The ships the Romans made were extremely strong. The largest were the grain carriers. These could also be used to transport people – up to 600 at a time. Flat-bottomed barges were used on the river and canals, ferrying goods from the large merchant ships that were too big to come upriver. Huge harbours were built all around the Mediterranean to provide docking areas and shelter for these large ships.

Building a ship

Roman shipbuilders built the keel of the ship first. After the keel had been laid, they carefully shaped planks for the hull and joined them edge-to-edge with mortise and tenon joints. They fitted strengthening ribs inside the frame, and then built the deck on top. The lower part of the hull was often cased in lead or treated with wax and tarred fabric to protect it from the so-called sea worms, a type of mollusc that bored into the wood.

Corbitas

The most common type of merchant ship was the *corbita*, a round-hulled ship with a curving prow and stern. Depending on its size, it could carry cargoes weighing between 70 and 350 tonnes. Although *corbitas* could only travel at about 3.5 knots, they still sailed as far as India to trade.

Lighthouses

A Roman lighthouse is shown at the top of this mosaic. The first Roman lighthouse was built in AD 50 at Ostia, the port near Rome. It was built on an artificial island, which the Romans created by filling the hulk of a ship with concrete. The Ostia lighthouse was the first in a network that was to be of great help to sea travellers. By AD 400, there were thirty lighthouses positioned at the entrances to harbours. The biggest used massive metal mirrors to focus the light from large fires.

War machines

The imperial Roman army was a well-equipped and highly disciplined force. It was used first to expand the Empire, by conquering neighbouring territory, and then to keep the peace within it. By the time of Julius Caesar, in the first century BC, the Roman army had become expert at laying siege. Its commanders could call up the finest artillery weapons of the time, and these included large and sophisticated catapults. The use of artillery in waging war was an idea the Romans had learned from the Greeks.

The *onager*

The *onager* was a catapult that was used to throw rocks or burning materials. The technology involved in making and using it had been adapted from the Greeks. It could throw a 50 kg boulder 400 m. This catapult is of a similar design.

A skein of cords was tightened around the throwing arm.

The arm was winched back.

Throwing arm

This hook was pulled away and the arm hurled its load forwards.

The *ballista*

The *ballista* was a smaller type of siege machine that fired arrows or iron bolts. It gave covering fire for the soldiers as they attacked. Towards the end of the first century AD, Dionysius of Alexandria invented an 'automatic *ballista*' – a catapult that carried a magazine of arrows. As each arrow dropped into a slot in the catapult, the bow string was released by a trigger, and the arrow was fired. The process continued until all the arrows had been used.

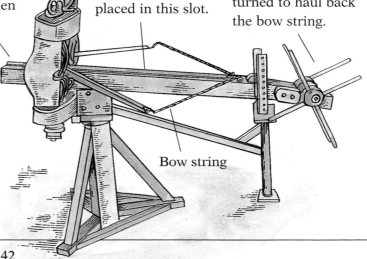

The arrow shot out here when the string was released.

The arrow was placed in this slot.

The winch was turned to haul back the bow string.

Bow string

Making a shield

A legionary soldier's shield was carefully constructed from thin sheets of wood, which were glued together, bound with iron or bronze around the edges and covered with leather. A metal boss at the centre protected the hand grip hollowed out at the back of the shield. You can make a replica shield very easily. You will need some stiff cardboard (a strong box from the supermarket will do). You will also need some glue to stick everything together, some paint and a paintbrush, coloured metal foil for decoration, scissors and tape.

1 Carefully cut out one side of the box for the shield and paint it. Red might be a good colour.

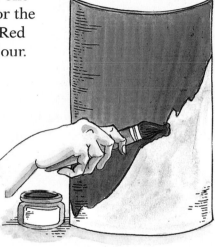

2 Cut two strips of cardboard from another part of the box and tape them to the back of the shield to make the hand grip.

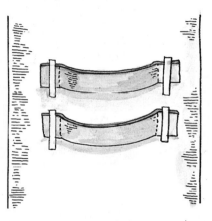

3 Cut out a circle of foil to make a central boss for your shield. Alternatively, cover a shallow plastic pot with foil and stick it to the shield to make the boss stand out.

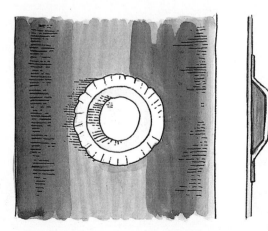

4 Decorate the front of the shield with coloured metal foil. Put some foil round the edges, like metal binding on a real shield.

Roman soldiers protected themselves by overlapping their shields in front of them and above their heads to form a barrier. This was called a *testudo*, from the Latin word for a tortoise or tortoise shell. Get some friends to make shields and form your own *testudo*!

Technology through time

Archaeological evidence helps historians to work out when a new form of technology was used. Pictures on mosaics, stone carvings, objects uncovered at the site of Roman towns and buildings – even the remains of the buildings themselves – can provide clues. Sometimes, descriptions of tools and techniques that were written by the Romans have survived in some form, and these are also an important source of evidence.

753 BC	This is the date when Rome is traditionally thought to have been founded.
c.500 BC	A Roman invents the safety pin. The idea is lost when the Roman Empire comes to an end, and is not rediscovered until the nineteenth century.
312 BC	Work begins on the Via Appia, a road that later runs from Rome to Brindisi on the coast of Italy. The Romans also begin to build their first aqueduct, the Aqua Appia, which brings water to Rome from springs 16 km away.
272 BC	The Aqua Anio aqueduct is built; for most of its 64-km length it runs underground.
264–241 BC	The First Punic War, against Carthage in North Africa, takes place. The Romans build their first warship.
c.200 BC	Concrete is first used, in the Roman town of Palestrina, in Italy. Three-storey apartments, called *insulae*, are built in Rome.
c.170 BC	The first paved roads are built in Rome.
144-140 BC	The 92-km Aqua Marcia is built. It is the first aqueduct to have long sections carried above ground on arches.
c.100 BC	Five-storey *insulae* are being built in Rome. Around this time, Roman engineers learn how to make domes. Glass skylights, the first window panes, are installed in the homes of wealthy people. The Romans also discover that a type of volcanic ash called *pozzolana* can be used to make superb waterproof concrete.
85 BC	Gaius Sergia Orata invents the *hypocaust* system for heating villas. Soon, public baths are heated in the same way.

The crane was an important piece of Roman technology. It made the construction of buildings, bridges and aqueducts much easier.

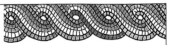

55 BC	Julius Caesar's troops build a wooden bridge across the River Rhine in just ten days.
19 BC	Marcus Agrippa builds the Pont du Gard aqueduct in Gaul (now France). It still stands today.
AD 1	Vitruvius describes the first known undershot water wheel in a book on architecture and engineering.
AD 60	The famous Roman writer Pliny the Elder describes a *vallus*, a harvesting machine pulled by oxen.
AD 70	The emperor Vespasian orders the building of the Colosseum. It will be the biggest theatre in the world until the twentieth century.
AD 122–6	Roman engineers and soldiers build Hadrian's Wall, to protect the Roman province of Britannia from attack by the tribes in what is now Scotland.
AD 130	The emperor Hadrian orders the building of the Pantheon, the shrine of all the gods, in Rome.
AD 230	The last of the major aqueducts supplying Rome is completed. The aqueduct carries 750 million litres of water to the city every day.
*c.*AD 400	The overshot water wheel is developed.

The invention of the overshot water wheel allowed water power to be used much more efficiently.

Glossary

Amurca The mushy substance that remained after the oil had been separated from the pulped flesh of olives during the making of olive oil.

Aqueduct A system of pipes and channels, either above or below ground, for moving water from one place to another.

Artillery Weapons, such as catapults, that are used to fire missiles.

Brazier A metal container in which fires were lit. It could be moved from room to room, or outside, to provide heat wherever it was needed.

Camber The upward curve of a road surface.

Cement Finely powdered stone used as a building material.

Concrete A strong building material, made by mixing cement, sand, stones and water.

Empire A group of countries or provinces under the rule of an emperor.

Forum The business and shopping centre of a Roman town. It usually had an open central square, surrounded by shops and offices.

Hypocaust An underfloor heating system used in wealthy homes and bath-houses.

Ingot A block of metal that has been melted and then shaped in a mould.

Mortar A mixture of cement, lime, water and sand used in building work to stick bricks or stone blocks together.

Mosaic A pattern made from thousands of tiny cubes of stone, glass or other materials, used to decorate walls and floors.

Ore Rock that contains metals.

Pier A brick or stone support for a wall or other building.

Pile A post that is driven into the ground to form part of the foundations of a building.

Ploughshare The blade on a plough that cuts through the soil.

Pozzolana Volcanic ash and dust used to make cement.

Province Part of a country or an empire.

Reaping Cutting a crop.

Smelt To obtain metal from ore by heating it.

Stopcock A valve used to control the flow of water in a pipe.

Treadmill A large wheel that people could stand inside and 'walk' round with their feet. It was used to provide power.

Winch A machine used to lift or lower loads by turning a rope or chain wound round a barrel. The rope is turned by hand or by a motor.

Further information

Books to read

Introduction to the Romans by Lesley and Roy Adkins (The Apple Press, 1991)
Look into the Past: The Romans by Peter Hicks (Wayland, 1993)
The Romans by Jacqueline Dineen (Heinemann, 1991)
The Romans: Fact and Fiction by Robin Place (Cambridge University Press, 1988)
What Do We Know About The Romans? by Mike Corbishley (Simon & Schuster Young Books, 1991)

Videos

The Romans and the Celts (*Eureka* series, Educational Television Company)
Video Plus: The Romans (BBC Educational Publishing)

Places to visit

British Museum, London
Fishbourne Roman Palace, Chichester, West Sussex
Hadrian's Wall, Northumberland and Cumbria
Roman Baths Museum, Bath, Avon

Acknowledgements

The recipe on p11 is from *The Classical Cook Book* by Sally Grainger (British Museum Press).
The photographs in this book were supplied by the following: Ace/Peter Adams 4–5; AKG/Erich Lessing title page, 12, 21; Ancient Art and Architecture Collection/R. Sheridan 6–10, /G. Garvey 31, /R. Sheridan 32, /Brian Wilson 33; Axiom/Jim Holmes 19; CM Dixon 13–15,17, 20, 22, 28, 36, 38–40, 41; Robert Harding/Simon Harris 25; Michael Holford 27, 29, 34, 35, 37, 41; Museum of London 16. The publishers have made every effort to contact copyright holders, but in cases where they have been unable to do so, would be happy to make the necessary arrangements at the first opportunity.

Index

Page numbers in **bold** indicate that there is information about the subject in a photograph or diagram.